Frontispiece: First period vase. 10″ high. A well-proportioned example of the use of a scale-blue ground, Kakiemon style of enamelling and honey gilding which typifies the splendour of the latter years of the period. *c.* 1770.

WORCESTER PORCELAIN

Stanley W. Fisher, F.R.S.A.

WARD LOCK & CO. LIMITED · LONDON

DEDICATION

To Nick and Betty Crane

ACKNOWLEDGMENTS

The author and publishers are indebted to the Worcester Royal Porcelain Co. Ltd. for the photographs reproduced in this book, and especially to Mr. W. B. Dunn, Managing Director, and Mr. H. Sandon, Museum Curator.

The cover illustration of Doves is reproduced by courtesy of the Antique Porcelain Co. Ltd.

The frontispiece illustration of a First Period Vase is reproduced by courtesy of Newman and Newman (Antiques) Ltd.

Printed in Great Britain by Cox & Wyman Limited

London · Reading · Fakenham

Set in Monotype Garamond

The Beginnings

To the collector the name of Worcester is synonymous with fine porcelain, from the beginning of the highest quality as regards design, potting and glazing, and decorated in such an amazingly wide variety of tasteful styles, Oriental, Continental and purely English according to period, that even nowadays previously unrecorded patterns occasionally appear in the sale-rooms.

In this book, which is introductory in character to the study of the wares of a concern whose history spans a period of over two hundred years, it is impossible to delve too deeply into origins which have been and still are being the subject of much scholarly research. We know, however, that on 4th June 1751 a Deed of Partnership was signed by fourteen gentlemen to form a company to make porcelain. Among the signatories the best known are Dr. John Wall, William Davis, and the brothers Richard and Josiah Holdship, and there is little doubt that Wall and Davis in particular had some practical (though in the case of the former, amateurish) knowledge of porcelain making, though in fact their greatest asset, when funds needed to be raised, was the possession of the knowledge, the equipment, the sources of supply of materials, and even the services of trained workmen from an already existing factory.

The factory in question was in Bristol, a building known as 'Lowdin's China House' in Redcliffe Backs owned by Benjamin Lund and William Miller. Here, during the late 1740's and until the sale to the Worcester company, a soft paste porcelain was made, containing Steatite or Soap-rock, and under the circumstances it is natural to find that this 'Lowdin's', 'Redcliffe Backs' or, more properly 'Lund's Bristol' porcelain is very similar in body, style and decoration to the earliest Worcester ware. The manufacture was merely removed from Bristol to Worcester, with the un-interrupted services of Robert Podmore and John Lyes who, according to Clause 20 of the articles of partnership, 'have for some time been employed by the inventors in the said Manufacture'. There is no real certainty whether porcelain making in Warmstry House, near to the cathedral, began in 1751 or 1752, but at any rate a comparison between undoubted, marked Bristol specimens and very early Worcester ones shows the same neat, careful potting, the same shapes, the use of clear-cut, dainty moulding, the same reticent underglaze blue painting, and of course the common use of Chinese designs rendered carefully in enamels of fine bright quality. The early steatitic paste is usually found to have a greenish translucency by transmitted light (though occasionally it may be almost colourless), and the clear glaze is never crazed. These two features are indeed characteristic of all Worcester during the first thirty years of manufacture, though the greenish colour, pro-nounced at first, tends to become nearer to the palest yellow in later specimens. Pieces of this change-over period do not bear ground colours, and it is rare to find any gilding.

Lund's Bristol is very popular among collectors, who base attribution upon the existence of a very few sauce and butter-boats bearing the name BRISTOLL or BRISTOL embossed in countersunk relief on the bases. Apart from purely domestic wares we may fairly definitely credit to Lund's factory a number of small hexa-gonal bottles with bulbous bases and long necks, and large (up to 14") vases with covers, painted in the Chinese style in a palette of brilliant blue, green, iron red, yellow and aubergine. A feature of this early enamelling is the painstaking delicacy of the brushwork, as if the outlines and details were drawn with a single hair.

The First Period, 1751-83

About 1751, then, began the 'Dr. Wall' or 'First Period' of Wor-cester porcelain making proper, and it lasted until 1783, seven years after Wall's death, when the former London agent, Thomas Flight, bought the business for his sons John and Joseph. The wares of the period are outstanding above all, perhaps, for an early mastery of technique, as shown by the neat potting of the fine, rather hard paste, the composition of which hardly varied throughout the years, a range of always pleasing but eminently practical shapes, and an astonishing wealth of decorative styles to which there seems no end. If we except the more splendid extravagances of the last ten years of the period (which even then were never vulgarly ostentatious) early Worcester decoration is comparatively reticent, seldom overcrowded so as to detract from the pure beauty of the paste, and always well placed, while at the same time often surprising the modern eye by the juxtaposition of seemingly clashing colours which yet seem to blend quite harmoniously.

Because the First Period paste and glaze was so uniform its identification is not really so difficult, even without the benefit of characteristic shape or pattern. The green translucency is not an infallible clue, however, for apart from the yellowish exceptions already mentioned, it must be remembered that the same characteristic is sometimes present in specimens of, for example, Liverpool or Longton Hall. The glaze is thin and clear, glistening, sometimes (but not always, as was once thought) shrinking away within the foot-rim, alternatively pooling into a mass of almost microscopic little bubbles, sometimes black-specked in very early pieces, but never crazed. The footrims of bowls, cups, saucers, plates and dishes are bluntly triangular in section, and handles are seldom askew. It is the exception to find firecracking or warping. As regards shapes, and remembering that silver shapes imitated at Worcester were available to every early factory, the collector quickly learns to recognize, for instance, the typical globular tea-pot with its flower-knobbed cover, the ovoid 'sparrow-beak' jug with gracefully curving loop handle, usually grooved, the mask-lipped 'cabbage-leaf' moulded jug, the ovoid tea-poy which looks so unbalanced and incomplete without its tiny little cover, and so forth. He learns to recognize the various beautiful mouldings so characteristic of the first ten years of the period, as exemplified on sauce-boats and tea wares. Table wares indeed always formed the greater part of early Worcester output, only a few exceedingly rare figures were made, and vases are not often seen, though they were made in various shapes and sizes. Among other decorative items we may include cornucopias, several kinds of trellis-sided, openwork baskets, ornamental tureens, and shell centrepieces. We

7

must not forget a wide range of so-called 'pickle-trays', moulded in the forms of scallop-shells or ivy leaves, and other table 'extras', such as salad bowls, cress dishes, egg-cups, mustard-pots, ladles and spoons, knife handles, egg drainers, patty-pans and funnels. Some of these smaller items are exceedingly rare.

Worcester Marks

Though much early Worcester is unmarked, the general use of marks was usual from the beginning. We find the crescent (drawn and open on painted wares, shaded or solid on printed ones), the fretted square (or 'square mark'), and the initial letter W in script, in block capital form, or in a rectangle. Some marks were borrowed

First Period Tureen and Cover. 17½″ long. Painted in underglaze blue. From the same mould as a white tureen dated 1751. T and F (reversed) mark. *c.* 1755.

from foreign wares, such as the Meissen crossed swords (with or without the figures 9 or 91 between the points) and various sets of pseudo-Chinese characters. All these were commonly applied in underglaze cobalt blue, even the crossed swords seen on pieces printed in overglaze black or painted overglaze in 'dry blue' enamel, but with these notable exceptions it is interesting to know that because the mark was applied by a decorator who had in his hand a blue-laden brush, it is quite rare to find a mark upon pieces decorated entirely in enamels. The collector should not be dismayed to find that an obviously matching tea-bowl and saucer bear two different marks, the crescent and the fretted square, for example, since it is common sense to suppose that they were taken from stock as and when required to make up a service.

In addition to those marks which may be classed as definite

First Period Tea Wares. Examples of painting in underglaze blue on early moulded pieces. Open crescents and workmen's marks. *c.* 1755–60.

factory marks, there is a wide range of tiny symbols, numerals and letters, in underglaze blue (but very occasionally in overglaze enamel) which are known as 'workmen's marks'. They are to be found upon those early pieces, painted in underglaze blue, which formed the greater output by far of the earlier years. The cobalt blue pigment was painted upon the fired biscuit, after which the glaze was applied and, of course, fired. The intention was clearly to imitate or even to rival in popularity the imported Chinese 'Blue Nankin' porcelains, and though it varies in tone (but never with any hint of violet) the Worcester underglaze blue is distinctive. Decoration was mostly in the Chinese style therefore, not only in underglaze blue but also in overglaze enamels, consisting of anglicized arrangements of Chinese figures mostly of the 'Long Eliza' (tall, slender women) type, landscapes with pagodas, exotic trees and fences, water scenes with boats, and floral or flowering shrub arrangements. These decorative schemes are often found in conjunction with various diapered or brocaded patternings.

Although most of the underglaze blue designs were indeed merely interpretations of the Chinese idiom, one occasionally sees exact copies of early eighteenth-century Chinese 'blue and white', such as the well-known but rare 'Eloping Bride' motif or the lovely arrangement of a Long Eliza panel reserved upon a ground intended to imitate the cracking ice of Spring, with scattered, white prunus blossoms fallen upon it. Also copied from the Chinese we find the use of a 'powder blue' ground (in which the pigment was blown upon the ware in powder form to produce a granulated appearance) upon which are reserved little fan-shaped and round panels containing landscapes and flower sprays.

Styles of Decoration

It was inevitable that the English factories should as time went on look elsewhere for inspiration, and the Oriental styles of decoration were followed by patterns of flowers in the Meissen style, and these in turn by various French styles such as the well-known 'Cornflower' pattern which was used also in printed form from about 1760. Printing in underglaze blue was adapted at about that time from the already perfected process of printing in overglaze black, sepia, and puce, and the result is recognizable by its mechanical perfection of line and the absence of washes of pigment, which had perforce to be imitated by the use of shading and cross-hatching. Most of the copper plates used to produce the transfers were especially engraved for the purpose – as for example the very common 'Pine-cone' or 'Strawberry' pattern – but a few of those intended for black printing, such as the 'Parrot and Fruit', were adapted to suit the new form. It must not be forgotten that much blue-printing on Worcester wares was done at the Shropshire Caughley factory, whose underglaze blue was inclined to have a violet tinge.

The great preponderance of Worcester blue and white does not mean that early enamel painting presented any great technical difficulty – there is nothing amiss in the even earlier Lund's Bristol enamelled wares – and at first we find the same emphasis on the

First Period Salad Bowl. 11″ diam. Decorated in underglaze blue printing, and in the centre the 'pine-cone' pattern. Hatched crescent mark. *c.* 1770.

Chinese styles, and the same choice of motifs. Also of Chinese origin was some delicate pencilling in black enamel, while from Japan came the inspiration for copies of the work of a family of potters named Kakiemon, in the forms of floral compositions, patterns of wheatsheaves and quails, and fabulous beasts and birds in a palette predominantly red and gold.

Soon after 1755, as we have seen in the case of blue and white, the influence of the great Meissen factory made itself felt. We find lovely little harbour scenes and landscapes, and a new style of flower painting in polychrome or in a dry-looking, vivid blue enamel ('dry blue') drawn in great detail with an exceedingly fine brush, and often appropriately accompanied by the crossed swords mark. The typical 'Meissner Blumen' are found either as loose arrangements or bouquets of flowers, or as separate detached sprigs. Often the two styles were combined – a tiny sprig or two judiciously placed beneath a handle or spout to supplement the main bouquet – and particularly lovely are the combinations of sprigs in pale purple with coloured landscapes or armorial shields, or with bouquets of flowers in polychrome. From Meissen also came the painting of naturalistic birds, figures in landscapes, and the use of rococo painted scrollwork.

The overglaze printing previously mentioned was introduced at Worcester about 1756, the prime mover being the engraver Robert Hancock. It is true that wares so treated lack colour, but there is something most attractive in the neatness and clarity of the designs upon the white paste. With the exception of armorial wares, the shields of which were sometimes printed in outline ready to receive colours, the process was rather surprisingly not used to any extent to assist the enameller, though it is generally accepted that a London decorator named James Giles purchased black-printed wares from Worcester, upon which his artists applied enamel painting and gilding.

An important event which had considerable influence upon Worcester decoration was the engagement in 1768 of painters from the closing Chelsea factory. This old concern had perhaps catered for a rather more sophisticated public than had the Worcester proprietors, and the inevitable result of the influx was the appearance of rich ground colours and elaborate gilding, allied to the colourful painting of flowers, birds, figures and landscapes. In May

First Period Sauceboat. 5¾″ long. A good example of haphazard placing of enamelled decoration upon a moulded body. *c.* 1760.

1769 the Worcester factory was able to advertise ground colours of mazarine blue, sky blue (or turquoise), several greens, purple and scarlet, in addition of course to the underglaze powder-blue, and to a yellow which was an earlier Worcester invention. On some of these grounds, underglaze blue, yellow, pink, red and purple, a scale pattern was worked, and other patterned grounds include gold stripes and shagreen. All these were further embellished with more or less elaborate gilding, the fine Worcester honey gilding produced by grinding up gold leaf with honey, rather dull, but capable of being burnished to a sheen which is never brassy.

Reserved upon the coloured grounds we find several different stock types of brushwork. Some Meissen flower painting persisted, but the Sèvres way of using festooned wreaths across shaped panels (and also across plain white grounds) replaced it in favour. Occasionally too the reserves were filled with Oriental flowers. The painting of brightly coloured, impossible 'exotic birds', derived from the Golden Pheasant, and painted in a number of styles by recognizably different artists, was greatly developed and is found mostly in conjunction with 'scale blue'. Most beautiful of all, and comparatively rare and costly, is the reserving upon a lovely claret ground of panels of Chinese figures in the style of the French engraver Jean Pillement.

The French influence is also to be seen at a rather later date in the formal but pleasing 'Hop Trellis' patterns, which feature red berries, trailing foliage, and the trellis-like 'hop poles' in association, usually, with shagreen or royal blue borders. Borders did in fact tend to become ever more elaborate, often showing the daring use of colour to which reference has already been made. On the other hand, in the 1770's there was a frequent use of a wide blue border, usually carrying a gilded patterning, associated with flower painting or with an urn en grisaille, sometimes garlanded with flowers.

Kakiemon designs persisted, but a more popular Oriental style was based upon a simple underglaze blue foundation of four radiating panels and an inner circle of blue enclosing a prunus blossom motif or a single 'mons' or chrysanthemum head. Upon this foundation was built a whole series of 'Japan patterns', some of them, as for example the 'Old mosaick Japan', splendidly diapered and richly gilt. A different class of Japan pattern features the use of a flat, rather dull rouge-de-fer (orange red) in place of the underglaze blue. In the opinion of many these Japans are uninteresting, however wide in variety, and rather to be classed, perhaps, with the equally formal 'Whorl' or 'Queen Charlotte' pattern of alternate spiral bands of red, white and blue, though here again there is more variety of pattern than is immediately apparent. On the other hand, there can be no doubt about the reticent splendour of the 'Joshua Reynolds' pattern, with its phoenix or 'Ho-Ho bird' in gay red, blue and yellow, perched upon a turquoise rock, a splendid example of the Worcester daring use of strong colour.

Fakes and Forgeries

At this juncture it might be appropriate to make some mention of the pitfall that besets the path of the collector of the very finest Worcester porcelain – the work of the forger or faker. Apart from the efforts of Samson of Paris, which are easily recognizable with practice by their hard, cold-looking paste, mechanical painting, brassy gilding, and fuzzy-looking, pale blue square marks, he has to contend with genuine pieces of First Period Worcester which have had further additional decoration added to them, or which have been cleverly repaired. The repairer has not of course done his specialized work with any intention to deceive, but when a piece changes hands in the sale-room or in the trade neither vendor nor purchaser is necessarily aware of it, and the danger is obvious. The experienced collector tests his purchases, preferably before he buys them, under the rays of an ultra-violet lamp, by the warmer feel of a restored part against the tip of his tongue, by the duller sound against his teeth, or by careful pressure with a steel point. Sometimes he looks for the slight but significant difference between the original glaze and the new substitute when the piece is held at an angle to a source of light. It is much more difficult, sometimes, to decide whether at some time or other a simply decorated specimen has been converted into a rare or expensive one by the addition of ground colours or elaborate polychrome decoration, because the piece was refired after the work was done. The pieces chosen for this kind of attention were usually undecorated, simply decorated in underglaze blue, or sparsely painted with enamels. To such ware the faker added, usually, apple-green or claret ground

15

colour, leaving the original enamelling alone or sometimes adding more. In the case of a piece bearing only a painted underglaze blue border upon a moulded surface, it was an easy matter to convert a value of a few shillings into many pounds by adding elaborate enamelling of flowers, insects and birds. These are but examples of the kinds of deception which are frequently encountered, and one always looks for signs of refiring in the shape of staining and blackening, roughness, severe iridescence, or bubbling. Ground colours were sometimes applied too thickly in an attempt to cover original decoration beneath, which nevertheless does occasionally still peep out from beneath, usually as tiny traces of underglaze blue, or may even show through. Faked claret and apple-green has a tendency to flake off, and it is well to remember that for technical reasons gilding is never found upon the genuine apple-green, but was always applied as close to it as possible.

We have no space here to delve deeply into the amazing variety of and diversity of First Period Worcester pattern, into the rarities and the unusual. We cannot however omit mention of the work of those who are known as 'outside decorators'. Apart from those many china painters who wandered from factory to factory, taking their styles and characteristic brushwork with them, many were employed at decorating studios in London and elsewhere, and though the earlier work on Worcester porcelain was almost certainly done inside the factory walls, after about 1760 a great deal of ware was sent away to be enamelled in the more splendid styles. The studio proprietor best known to modern collectors was James Giles of Cockspur Street and later of Berwick Street, London, and it is possible to recognize the work of some of his staff. Thus, there is a distinctive class of exotic birds painted with a full brush; another with dishevelled plumage which we call the 'agitated bird'; landscapes with figures, in green and black; 'sliced' fruit, extremely well-painted; large flowers, armorial bearings and, of course, the overpainting of black-printed or blue-painted wares already mentioned. These classes of decoration are often accompanied by rich ground colours and fine gilding, but underglaze blue grounds, such as scale blue, were applied and fired in the high-temperature factory kilns before the ware was sent to London.

Most of Giles's workmen are known only by nickname – the 'sliced fruit painter' for example – but the 'Fable painter', whose renderings of Aesop's Fables are to be found on Worcester and other porcelains is known to have been Jefferyes Hamett O'Neale. Another outside worker who lived in London was John Donaldson, who specialized in classical figure subjects which are to be seen notably upon more important vases made about 1770.

Flight and Chamberlain, 1784-1850

Dr. Wall died in 1776, but Davis carried on until his death in 1783 when the works was bought by Thomas Flight. It might be thought that his sons, John and Joseph, would have found little difficulty in carrying on where Davis had left off, but although at first the old styles of ware were continued, as regards shape and decoration, the powerful rivalry of the Potteries, with their new bone-ash pastes and purely English styles of decoration, forced them to experiment. Indeed, such were the ensuing technical and labour problems that in 1788 some consideration was given to the possibility of moving the business to South Wales. However, this was not done, and through a series of partnerships Flights porcelain was made at Worcester until a merger took place in 1840 with the Chamberlain concern, about which we shall speak later.

I do not think it is necessary to pay overmuch attention to the changes of partnership. Briefly, they were as follows. One of the Flights, John, died in 1791, Joseph Flight and Martin Barr (Flight and Barr) 1792–1807, Barr, Flight and Barr (Martin's son) 1807–13, Flight, Barr and Barr 1813–40, Martin Barr senior having died in 1813.

Most of the Flights porcelain bears marks painted, printed or impressed, and all are reliable for dating purposes, with the exception of the crescent. This smaller version of the original mark (not always accompanied by the word FLIGHT or the word with a crown) was painted in underglaze blue. Despite its smaller size, its presence upon, for example, pieces decorated in scale blue and birds made by Flights about 1783 to 1790 may deceive the unwary if the chalky whiteness of the paste, the mechanical nature of the painting, and the substitution of flatter, more brassy mercury gilding for the old honey gilding are not taken into consideration. The same caution applies also to early Flights scale blue patterns marked with a rather bold, all too vivid square mark.

17

From the beginning efforts were made to improve the quality of the paste. Valentine Green, in his 'History of Worcester' published in 1796, mentions the 'improvements made in the texture of the ware in the year 1795', and indeed there is a common but unfounded belief that pieces made of a new, harder and whiter paste introduced by Martin Barr can be identified by the presence of an incised B mark. With the change in paste – a change not for the better so far as the collector is concerned – came a quite revolutionary change in style of decoration, for which there were several reasons. In the first place, a new school of landscape painting, inspired largely by Derby, was quickly adopted by the Stoke factories, and much Flights porcelain carries carefully painted views of Malvern Priory, Witley Court, Worcester Bridge and other local places of interest. The making of magnificent services lavishly painted and richly gilded was encouraged and indeed made necessary by frequent visits to the factory by royal and noble personages, of which a typical example is that made for the Duke of Clarence, superbly painted en grisaille with figures of Hope on the seashore by James Pennington. Many of the factory artists (for the outside decorator was seldom employed) were employed at various times by both the Flights and Chamberlain factories, being by now paid by time and not on piece-work rates, a change which naturally encouraged careful workmanship. Thomas Baxter, for instance, painted his meticulous panels of shells and feathers at Worcester before moving on to Swansea, only to return in 1819. Before he joined the Worcester decorating staff he had been principal of a school of art in the city, and among his pupils who later followed his example the names of Lowe and Cole are on record. Other Flights artists known to us by name and style are Moses Webster (who also worked at Derby), painter of naturalistic flowers, Astles, Richards and Stinton, also flower painters, Rogers, Doe, Silk and Robert Brewer, landscape painters, Barker, shell painter, and Davis, who painted exotic birds. The work of these artists is to be seen not only on services, but also upon cabinet cups and saucers, vases, and other sometimes most elaborate decorative pieces which were made in great variety. In fact, the time had come when the porcelain body was but a vehicle for fine painting which rather than paste is the preoccupation of collectors of Flights porcelain.

The making of blue and white was practically given up amidst

Chamberlains Cup and Saucer. A lovely example of restrained, tasteful decoration, in botanical style, on domestic ware. *c.* 1815.

this emphasis on ornamentation, one of the few exceptions being the blue 'Royal Lily' or 'Queen's Pattern' chosen by Queen Charlotte on her visit to the works in 1788, and not to be confused with the First Period 'Whorl' pattern. Japan patterns continued in favour, but the new styles, the so-called 'Derby Japans', were really revivals of the red, blue and gold Japanese Imari porcelains, sadly formalized, crowded and rather vulgar, though even at that rather less debased at Worcester than elsewhere.

It is futile to compare the products of Flights and of the First Period, if only because they must be judged by entirely different standards. In the space of thirty years taste changed from the rococo to the classical, from the carefree to the sophisticated, influenced no doubt as far as ceramics are concerned by Wedgwood and, to a lesser extent, by Derby. Apart from shape, though many of the same decorative subjects were continued, the treatment completely changed, resulting in a stiffness that resulted from meticulous care in drawing, colours that were harder and lacking in the subdued harmony that was such a feature of the early years, and the unfortunate tendency of the Regency taste to insist upon covering the entire surface of the ware.

Robert Chamberlain, said to have been the first apprentice at Dr. Wall's factory, left it in 1783 when the business changed hands to found his own factory, that was at first merely an enamelling establishment. This was in King Street, but by 1792 his new factory near the cathedral, where the present works now stands, was practically finished, and the decoration of wares mostly bought from Turner of Caughley was in full swing. Once again, we are not here concerned overmuch with the changes of partnership that took place – Chamberlain, his son Humphrey and Richard Nash until 1804, Humphrey and Robert Chamberlain, with Gray Edward Boulton 1804 to 1811, Humphrey and his son Robert 1811 to 1827, John Lilly and Walter Chamberlain as Chamberlain and Co. from 1828 to 1840. The company was then merged with Flight, Barr and Barr.

One must assume that the actual making of porcelain began when the new factory was completely equipped. The body then perfected is rather grey, with sometimes a slightly wavy surface, covered with a glaze that sometimes crazed. Apparently there was less experiment than at Flights, the only noteworthy innovations being a special body known as the 'Regent', in 1811, and a very opaque, almost a 'stone china', made towards the end of the century. At best the Regent paste compares favourably with the best of Welsh porcelain, and it was probably almost as expensive to produce, since its use was limited to the making of special orders. Fortunately, most Chamberlains porcelain is clearly marked, and the collector is well-advised to be cautious against the blind acceptance as Chamberlains Worcester of unmarked pieces, always with the proviso that it was common Chamberlain practice to mark only the lid of a tea-pot or sucrier of a tea service, or a few dishes of a dessert service.

Much that has been said of the rival Flights concern applies also to Chamberlains, the advantages of visits by Royalty and the nobility, the emphasis on ornamental wares, and the changes in style, though in fact I have always thought that the decoration of Chamberlains porcelain is on the whole rather more conservative. So far as domestic wares are concerned we find the same familiar spirally fluted forms – the Chamberlain rib being double or ribbed whereas that on Flights wares is single – and the same simple sprigged decoration in blue or sepia and gold. Scale patterns with flowers or exotic birds and Japan patterns were continued, the latter in very gaudy forms. We find also the frequent use of a particularly strong, shimmeringly uneven mazarine blue as the ground for panels of flower painting.

The Chamberlain painting staff included Davis for birds, Wood, Doe, Rogers and Williams for landscapes, Steel for fruit, Plant for heraldry and Baxter for figure subjects, many of them taken from Shakespeare. We have previously said that some of these also worked for Flights. One of the best of the painters was Humphrey Chamberlain, junior, who unfortunately died in 1824, and who was remarkable for his minutely careful brushwork.

The 'Kerr and Binns Period', 1851-61

The new company which was formed by the amalgamation of the rival concerns, in 1840, did not succeed as well as had been expected. There were quarrels, resulting in several changes of partnership before, in 1851, what is known as the Kerr and Binns period began. The partners were W. H. Kerr (related by marriage to the Chamberlains) and R. W. Binns. Kerr was the businessman, while Binns was responsible for the artistic direction. Spurred on by the imminence of the Dublin Exhibition planned for 1853 and encouraged by the success of the Great Exhibition, the partners made every effort to revive the somewhat faded glories of Worcester porcelain, engaging new artists while retaining the services of some of the old, such as Plant, Williams and Doe. Among the new-comers was the son of a well-known Dublin sculptor named Kirk, who designed a remarkable dessert service for twenty-four persons, the comports supported by figures from the Midsummer Night's Dream. This 'Shakespeare Service', as it was called, undoubtedly brought the factory once again to the forefront by reason of its fine design and technical perfection.

The designers were greatly helped by the many noblemen and county gentlemen who were pleased to lend works of art to serve as models for ornamental wares. For example, the beauty of Limoges enamels inspired the lovely pâte-sur-pâte work of Thomas Bott, basically the laying in various thicknesses and degrees of opacity of a white enamel upon a dark cobalt blue ground. In readiness perhaps for a projected 1862 London Exhibition experi-ment began in the making of an entirely new body of soft ivory tone, which was at first treated in the Capo-di-Monte style under the name of 'Raphaelesque porcelain' but which was later adapted, as we shall see, to other foreign styles.

The Modern Company, 1862 to the Present Day

In 1862 the final change in the composition and name of the Worcester manufactory came about with the founding of the joint stock company which is still known as the Worcester Royal Porcelain Company Limited, a change which may be looked upon as incidental as far as we are concerned, since production and the development of style continued without interruption. Thus, more and more emphasis was placed on decoration, on fine specialized painting allied to splendid ground colours and lavish gilding. Wealthy patrons lent their old masters and other paintings to be copied, so that we find miniature representations of the work of Birkett Foster rusticity done by Joseph Williams and of Landseer animals by Robert Perling. Some of this sort of decoration was applied to white porcelain, but it was the ivory body which received most attention, since its intrinsic beauty both enhanced and was enhanced by enamelling. Thus, apart from the specialized painting, we find the successive influence of those foreign styles to which the ivory body was clearly suited. Just as a hundred years earlier the taste was for anything Chinese, so in the 1860's Japanese art was the rage. Binns began with a series of vases illustrating in low relief the work of the Japanese potter, and these were followed by pieces decorated with panels of various tints of bronze, silver and dusted gold, with scaled dragons and dainty piercing. Then followed pieces made and decorated in the Persian, Florentine, Italian and Louis XVI manner, all finely modelled and richly gilt, all technically perfect, but all, perhaps, too elaborate for modern taste, though it is interesting to note that at the Vienna Exhibition of 1873 the company tied with the Minton firm for the highest award. Mention must be made of the remarkable perforated or reticulated pieces made in the 1890's by George Owen, lace-like, delicate and fragile, with every tiny shaped aperture separately pierced. The finest examples of this kind of work include double-walled pieces, the inner wall solid and the outer pierced, and often brilliantly enamelled. Owen's pieces are usually signed, but cheaper imitations of them were mechanically produced.

The later Worcester wares of this century are familiar enough to need little description. The many specialized painters of Highland cattle, pheasants, swans, fruit and flowers are known because they signed their work, which is always accompanied by more or less elaborate gilding, applied by means of transfer on less expensive pieces. There have been from time to time, encouraged by the late Dyson Perrins, revivals of some of the earlier styles, though naturally enough extensive use has been made of transfer printing, a process which must inevitably be extended as the old painters die out with few young ones to replace them. One branch of porcelain making which is, however, flourishing as never before is the making of figures. Whereas during the First Period a mere handful of exceedingly rare models were made, and Chamberlains did little better, a very wide range of large and small models, in the ivory body and in highly glazed white beautifully enamelled with delicate colours have been produced by the present company, culminating in the exquisitely modelled Doughty birds and Lindner horses which will undoubtedly become the priceless antiques of the future.

Other Worcester Concerns

There remains yet a third outstanding Worcester factory, the wares of which have been much underrated, despite the fact that it had a long life. Thomas Grainger founded his works in 1800, in St. Martin's Street. Four years later his company was known as Grainger, Lee and Co., and when Grainger died in 1839 to be succeeded by his son George the name changed finally to G. Grainger & Co. At first most of the porcelain was made for Mortlocks, the London china dealers, whose name often appears instead of a factory mark. Indeed, much Grainger ware is unmarked, and much of it often passes as Chamberlains, because it was decorated in much the same style.

The copying of the various styles of the main factory continued right up to the time when in 1889 the two were amalgamated. Common to both were Parian wares, pâte-sur-pâte, and inferior imitations of Owen's pierced ware. The collector of Graingers porcelain cannot do better than to examine examples of it in the Worcester Works Museum, now newly and beautifully housed, for much is of a quality equal to anything made by Chamberlains or Flights, though usually unrecognized because unmarked.

It was natural that others should follow Chamberlain's example and strike out on their own in a city which had such a reputation for porcelain making. Thus, in 1875 a modeller named James Hadley founded his own design and modelling concern, until 1894, at first to cater for the Royal Worcester Company, and thereafter to make his own wares. His 'Hadley Ware' is similar in style to that of the parent factory, with much use of the ivory body, but it is usually distinguished by the regular use of coloured clay enrichments in relief, usually of a most distinctive bluish-green colour, allied to floral painting in colours or in monochrome. Some pleasing landscape painting is to be seen on plates with rococo, moulded edges. The Hadley company was taken over by the main factory in 1905.

A small and comparatively unimportant factory was founded by another Worcester employee named Edward Locke in 1895, its products being rather inferior copies of the typical ivory wares of the period. They are invariably marked, and indeed the factory was closed about 1904 as the result of legal action by the Royal Worcester Company against Locke's use of the name WORCESTER in his mark.

In spite of the fact that every nineteenth-century porcelain factory of any importance had its own staff of skilled painters, there was still room for the outside decorator, who purchased his wares in the undecorated state from any available source, painted them, and added his own mark. Many pieces of Chamberlains Worcester (and of Coalport too) bear the name of Sparks (George Sparks) who worked in the city from 1836 to 1854, before becoming the London agent for the Royal Worcester Company, and Enoch Doe and George Rogers were Worcester painters who became outside decorators and whose work is usually marked with their names.

It will be seen from this short account of porcelain making in Worcester that the scope for the collector is virtually endless. Whether he decides to concentrate upon period, factory, or style there is something to suit every taste, and the rising costs of fine specimens present the only obstacle to his indulgence. The illustrations in this book may serve to help him to decide what he likes best, and thereafter there is no lack either of collections or of specialized literature to help him to further his pursuit. Indeed, no other kind of English porcelain has received so much attention, and it is my hope that this introduction may perhaps indicate some of the reasons why.

Graingers Vase. 8″ high. One of a pair, perhaps painted by Baxter, of fine
quality. Marked 'Grainger Lee & Co. Worcester' in red script. *c.* 1830.

SPECIAL SERVICES
Details of Special Services made by Flights
Period 1789–1836

1789   DUKE OF CLARENCE, the King's fourth son, created Duke of Clarence and St. Andrew, and invested with the Order of the Thistle. A service was ordered in honour of the event, in the Sèvres style, in the centre H.R.H. arms without supporters, properly emblazoned, with a border of entwined ribbons of the two orders, forming panels enclosing roses and thistles.

1792   DUKE OF CLARENCE. In the centre of each piece a figure of Hope with an anchor, symbolizing the Duke's naval connections, with a border of royal blue richly gilt. Painted by James Pennington.

1805   ROYAL SERVICE. In the centre of each piece the Royal Arms, the royal blue border a pattern of the union device in gold arranged in panels, enriched with oak-leaves and laurel. A similar service, but more elaborately gilt, was made for the Prince of Wales at the same time.

1806   SIR ROBERT PEEL. A service with full armorial bearings.

1807   DUKE OF GLOUCESTER. A service was made following upon a visit to the factory.

LORD VALENTIA. In the centre of each piece a landscape, copied from the drawings of a Mr. Page, with a border of alternate Greek anthemion and lotus in raised white on a gold ground.

1814   EMPEROR OF RUSSIA. The order followed a visit to the works by the Grand Duchess of Oldenburg. The service was decorated in the Empire style, with the Imperial Arms in the centre, and a rich dark blue border, with scrolls and trophies in raised gold.

NABOB OF OUDE. A design of a central landscape with a dancing girl, painted by Baxter, with a border of rich, leafy scrollwork in gold, broken at the top by a coat of arms.

1816   PRINCESS CHARLOTTE. A breakfast service made for her wedding, designed with flowers in the centre, with an apple-green border containing three large and three small reserves containing flowers and flies on an ivory-coloured ground.

1823   LORD AMHERST. On his appointment as Governor General of India. The central coat of arms is of large size, in proper colours, in the style encouraged by Georges III and IV and William IV. The borders are in Saxon green, with solid gold gadrooned edges and delicate gilt borders ornament also the inner rim. According to Binns, the accession of Queen Victoria brought a change to the use of smaller crests, arms and monograms upon armorial china.

1831 WILLIAM IV. Worcester shared with other factories, including Rockingham, the honour of making special services on the occasion of the King's accession to the throne. This Worcester example is heraldic in character, with a dark blue ground upon which are three large and three small reserves containing paintings of jewels of the Orders of the Garter. St. George and Dragon, the Thistle and St. Patrick, Bath, St. Michael, and the Guelphic Order. In the centre are the Royal Arms of England. A feature is delicate gold tracery, with white enamel beads to represent pearls.

1836 WILLIAM IV to the IMAUM OF MUSCAT. This presentation service is decorated with a design featuring a central motif of one of the Royal yachts, the 'Prince Regent', bordered in green upon a heavily gilt gad-rooned edge, with the Imaum's crest at the top. It is said that the Imaum would have preferred a steam vessel, in exchange for a small teak-built battleship which he had given to the King.

Details of Special Services made by Chamberlains Period 1796–1811

1796 H.R.H. PRINCE OF ORANGE.

1802 LORD NELSON and LADY HAMILTON. Orders by both followed a visit to the factory. Lord Nelson ordered a dinner and a breakfast service, but only the latter was finished, because of his death. The design featured a central coat of arms with a Japan border. Many French copies of these services are known.

1806 DUKE OF CUMBERLAND. A breakfast service, in the same style as the Lord Nelson service.

1807 PRINCE OF WALES. At a visit to the works the Prince ordered a full service, each piece of a different pattern in, according to the local press, 'the most highly finished Oriental and Dresden designs'.

1811 PRINCE REGENT. In the Japan style, every piece different, and so known as a 'Harlequin' set. This set was made during the period 1811–1816, and the total cost was £4,047 19s. od. Some pieces bear fine paintings of dead game, figures and landscapes by Humphrey Chamberlain.

N.B. The accompanying reproduction is of a list of some of the pieces evidently packed on Dec. 21st, 1815, given to me by the late Dyson Perrins. On the reverse of the page are the words 'Red Ink in London, Black Ink Paperd in Worcester, Pencil Mark in the Warehouse'.

1816 PRINCESS CHARLOTTE. Chamberlains received large orders in readiness for the wedding of the Princess. The design of the dessert service was a modification of an old Sèvres style, featuring flowers in the centre on a drab ground, and panels in which were embossed the rose, thistle and shamrock. The dinner service was richer in style, of a delicate grey colour, with elaborate gilding and exotic birds in six diamond-shaped reserves. In the centre were bouquets of flowers.

1818   EAST INDIA COMPANY. For use at the Madras Presidency, when the Corporation was at the height of its power. In the centre of the design was the coat of arms in proper colours, surrounded by burnished gold arabesques upon a salmon-pink ground. Another and larger service was ordered, less elaborately decorated, for general use, and the total cost of the two was £4,190 4s. od.

GRAND DUKE MICHAEL. A service made of the 'Regent' paste, upon each piece a view of some mansion or town visited by the Duke on his tour. Artists were employed to paint these subjects from nature, and the service had to be ready in twelve months. The paintings were in oblong panels reserved upon a salmon-pink ground covered with a rich gold marbled patterning.

1820   GEORGE IV. A service made of the 'Regent' paste was ordered on the occasion of the King's accession. Each piece had a brilliant green border which showed to best advantage upon this particularly fine porcelain, with three reserves painted with flowers, and in the centre were the Royal arms.

Appendix B

PAINTERS AND GILDERS AT CHAMBERLAINS
Period 1799–1804

The following names are taken from the Painting Wage Book, which covers the period February 1799 to July 1804.

John Ash	Thomas Pegg
Ralph Bell	John Redgrave
Joseph Birbeck	John Rickhus
William Birbeck	George Rogers
John Bly	James Rogers
George Chamberlain	John Scarratt
Gilbert Crump	John Sherrett
T. Frame	John Stevenson
John Hewett	William Stephenson
William Hewett	Charles Toulouse
John Keeling	John Toulouse
Alexander Langdale	James Turner
William March	Richard Walthall
C. Mills	Joseph Yarnold
Robert Mills	Joshua Yeates

Appendix C

GRAINGER PATTERN BOOKS

A number of pattern books of the Grainger company has survived, a study of which is of considerable help in the identification of unmarked pieces, particularly since many of the patterns are reproduced.

Pattern Book of Door Furniture and Cane Knobs

Comprising coloured illustrations of door knobs, key plates, finger plates and cane knobs, with dimensioned sketches. Shapes are both plain and rococo, with considerable use of ground colours, with some sea-weed patterns. The ground colours, which are to be found also on other Grainger wares, include bleu-celeste, sea green, match green, pink, cane, bisque, ultramarine, antwerp blue, silver grey, imitation marble, maroon, dark biscuit blue, enamel blue, white, dove marble, and Torqua green (a fine turquoise).

Three General Pattern Books

  1. Numbers 391–2000
  2. Numbers 1230X–2000X
  3. Numbers 2/1–2/506   Altogether 2885 patterns

It is impossible to date any pattern, but it is noteworthy that increasing use was made of printing, especially batt printing, with noted alternate colour schemes in the Spode manner. Much use was made of set border designs in combination with different styles of painting, especially of flowers and landscapes.

Use of Printing

The pattern book pages are illustrated with the actual prints used on the porcelain, with colour washes added. The following points are noteworthy:—

  1. Frequent use was made of batt-printed borders, particularly of an all-over pattern of flower heads on a dotted ground. One note reads 'Spriggs printed in strong bronze and part filled in'.

  2. Many printed sea-weed patterns, always by the batt process, 'printed in slate'.

  3. Elaborate chinoiseries, batt-printed, and washed in with coloured enamels.

  4. Printing often in mouse, dark blue, bronze and slate.

  5. An unusual but effective use of an outline composed of tiny circles for foliate and floral patterns, even for such detail as the veins of leaves.

  6. An ever-increasing use of printing for pattern outline.

Painters

There is a great preponderance of floral patterns, and frequent mention either of 'flowers by women' or 'men's flowers'. Artists are occasionally mentioned by name in connection with repetitive patterns, though it is to be supposed that any of them might be called upon to undertake the painting of special landscape or other individual designs. A list of these named painters is as follows:—

Bullock J.	Landscapes
Cotterill A.	Ground colours
Daniel J.	Landscapes
Daniel Wm.	Gilding
Evans Jno.	Wild flowers and sprays of roses, also geometrical arabesques
Evans	'Japan birds'
Freeman	'Dotted gold' grounds
Freeman	Flowers
Graney	Fine delicate flowers
Grainger Geo.	Roses with brown leaves
Hathaway C.	Gilding, especially intricate arabesque ornament
Hewitt Mrs.	'Flowers done by Mrs. Hewitt', particularly wreaths of roses
Jones Mrs.	Matt purple sprigs
Low	Flower sprays
Lucas	Gilding
Lulman G. H.	Key patterns, and 'twisted patterns'
May	Birds and ground colours
May Wm.	Sketchy flower sprays in conventional style, built up on a single curving stem, with a little spray or blossom in every curve, and a single leaf or blossom at either end. Also intricate geometrical border patterns
Meigh	Flowers
Norris	Flowers
Parry	Flowers
Rickhurst	Large red leaves and grapes
Rickhuss	Flowers, mostly conventional in Japan style
Rickhuss	Birds
Rickus	'Slight Japan' patterns
Roden Margaret	Flowers and blue sprigs
White	Puce flower sprays
Wood Stanley	Roses and small sprigs, large single flowers

Packed for His Royal Highness
The Prince Regent Dec 21
1815

1 Oval Table Tureens & Stands
12 Sauce do ———— do —
10 doz Table plates
2,4 7½ doz Soup do —
10 dishes 10 In
11, do — 12 In
4,1,4 do — 14 In
1,6 do — 15
1,0 do — 16.
3. 5 do — 18
3, 3 do — 20 In
14 Pincushion dishes Small Size
6 do — do large
11 Square dishes
2, 4 Round dishes 11¼
7. 7 do — 11½
5, 4 do — 12
3 do — 12½
1 Round Tureen
2 Stands

Deficient of His Royal Highness
Order
1 Round Tureens & Stands & Cover
2 Vegetable dishes complete
2 doz Table plates
½ doz Soup " "
18 dishes 14 In
1, 2 " — 15
3 — 18
2 5 — 20, 1
3 " — 22
4, 10 Round dishes 11¼
" — 11½
4 " — 12
0 Pincushion dishes large
3 Square s — Blue Ground

Chamberlains 'Prince Regent' Service. A packing list for part of the 'Japan Harlequin' service made between 1811 and 1816, at a cost of £4,047.19.0. (see Appendix)

Chamberlain–Caughley Co. working A page from a Chamberlain record, listing goods purchased 'in the white' or blue-printed, from Thos Turner of Caughley (see Appendix)

48789

			£	S	D
Augst 26 Goods Recd from Thos Turner Esqr			£	S	D
No 203 1 B Otk Plate 1o Bf d White			..	1	3
2 Do 2o N d Do	1/9		..	3	6
2 Do 1o Dresden Flower	1/6		..	3	..
2 Upright Ewers 2o Do	2/		..	4	..
24 Cups 1o Dagger Border	/5		..	10	..
1 Bute Teapot 4o Do	..		..	4	..
2 Upright Ewers 2o Do	2/		..	4	..
12 Coffees Do	/10		..	10	..
4 Sau 1o Com Blue Bord	4/6		..	1	6
1 Canister Do Do	1/9		..	1	9
2 Pint Basons Daggr Border	1/6		..	3	..
5 Saucers 2o Basket Chantilly Sprig	1/9		..	3	9
20 Do 2o Temple	/7		..	11	8
3 Caudle Stands White	1/		..	3	..
3 Caudle Cups Dresden Flower	2/6		..	7	6
2 Do Stands Do	1/6		..	3	..
1 Caudle Do Royal Stripe	2/6		..	2	6
1 Upright Ewer 2o Blue Border			..	2	..
3 Mellons 1o White	2/6		..	7	6
2 Shells 1o Do	2/		..	4	..
2 Reddish Dishes Do	2/		..	4	..
8 Desert Plates 3o Do	1/		..	8	..
33 Cups 1o Brosley White	6/6		..	17	10½
19 Saucers 1o Do Do	6/6		..	10	3½
2 Sugar Boxes Do Do	1/9		..	3	6
10 B Otk Plates 1o Do Do	1/3		..	12	6
9 Do 2o Do Do	1/9		..	15	9
Card Over			8	2	10

Appendix D

CHAMBERLAIN INVOICE BOOKS

Among the invoice books which have survived, covering the period
c. 1788–1843, several relate to dealings between the Chamberlains and
Turner of Caughley. It is clear that in addition to the fact that a great deal
of ware was obtained from Caughley, either in the white or partly or
wholly decorated, to be finished at Worcester or even sold as Worcester
without any additional decoration having been placed upon it, the Worcester company did occasionally send ware to Caughley to be decorated.
Thus, we find an entry which reads as follows:—

> Feb. 6th. 1789.
>> To Thos. Turner Esq.
>> For painting a 'red border' on 11 pieces   3/10
>> For gilding the same   4/3

The accompanying illustration of a page of an invoice book which is
dated Aug. 26th, 1789 gives some indication of the variety of ware
purchased from Caughley.

The books contain a number of interesting comments which were
evidently included in letters written to Turner. The following are typical.

Aug. 23rd 1789.   'Hope I have seen the last of Raddish Dishes and
Centres, the last is a most terrible shape to my taste
and what is more I have often had the mortification
to have my opinion confirm'd by a great dislike. No
more mustard pots those that we have there is no
spoons sent for them.'

Sept. 4th 1789.   'Please to send no more white seconds till further
orders as at present we really want room to put them.'
'I am sorry to inform Mr. Turner it is now three
months since I order'd . . . they are for a lady in
Gloster who I am apprehensive must by this time be
greatly affected at our delay.'

WORCESTER PORCELAIN
1750-1947

Plate 1. Dr. John Wall, M.D. 1708–76.

Plate 2. Lund's Bristol Vase. 9″ high. An obvious copy of a Chinese piece, even to the total lack of perspective in the drawing. The photograph clearly shows the typical 'spotted' treatment of the green wash of the foreground. *c.* 1750–52.

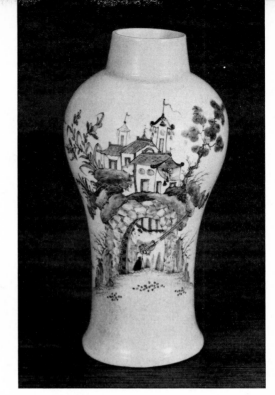

Plate 3. Lund's Bristol Sauceboat. 7½″ long. One of the two main types, and inspired by a silver shape. Other examples are known with the moulded decoration of festoons of fruit and ribbon bows accompanied by enamelled flower-sprays, or with the moulding itself coloured. Mark, BRISTOLL in relief. *c.* 1750.

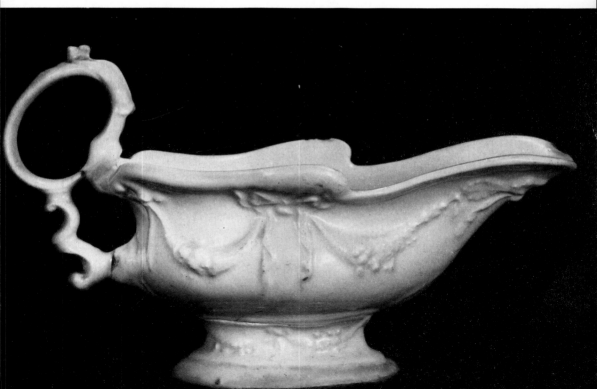

Plate 4. A pair of Lund's Bristol Vases. $6\frac{1}{2}''$ high. The baluster shape is typical, and the enamelled decoration in Chinese style is brilliant and beautifully detailed. The placing of some kind of secondary floral ornament on the opposite side of a piece was a common Worcester device.
c. 1750.

Plate 5. A Group of Lund's Bristol. The vase is $4\frac{1}{2}''$ high. Such dainty wares, brilliantly and finely enamelled as with a single hair of the brush, exemplify at an early date the tastefulness which marked the porcelains of the First (Dr. Wall) Period. They are also proof that good enamelling presented no real problem to the pioneers of porcelain making in Worcester. The decoration is Oriental in origin, and the pieces may be dated *c.* 1750–52.

Plate 6. Lund's Bristol or Early Worcester Tea-pot. 6″ high. A very lovely tea-pot of the change-over period, painted in brilliant enamels with a pattern commonly known as the 'Beckoning Chinaman'. The same Oriental design is often seen upon bell-shaped and cylindrical tankards, accompanied, as upon this specimen, by a group of peonies on the other side of the piece. *c.* 1750–55.

Plate 7. First Period Sauceboat. 6½″ long. A simplified version of the Lund's Bristol model, painted in underglaze cobalt blue with Chinese water-scenes and flowers. The same model sometimes bears other forms of decoration, both in underglaze blue and enamels, the main motif being fitted carefully to the moulded reserve. Marked with a painter's symbol of a swastika. *c.* 1755.

Plate 8. First Period Bleeding Bowl. 5¼″ diam. A collector's rarity, painted in underglaze blue with trailing leaves and tendrils, and curious snail-like creatures which were probably inaccurately copied from the Chinese. The handle typifies the usual fine early Worcester moulding, clear and crisp. Painter's mark. *c.* 1755.

Plate 9. First Period Tea-pot. 4″ high. An unusually small but typically shaped tea-pot with the distinctive open rose-bud cover knob and plain loop handle. The underglaze blue decoration by a workman known for obvious reasons as the 'cannon ball painter' is a common one on wares of this period, though the trellis border is to be seen upon the wares of other early factories, notably Liverpool. On the base is the inscription 'W.M. 1766'.

Plate 10. First Period Dessert Plate. 8½″ diam. The purely Chinese style of decoration, in underglaze blue, is painted in fair imitation of a Chinese original in a blue which well copies the true K'hang Hsi sapphire blue. The pattern has been given the name of the 'Hundred Antiques'. Antiquity is reverenced by the Oriental, and the various articles in the decoration have ancient religious or mythological significance. The mark also is a copy of a Chinese one. *c.* 1760.

Plate 11. First Period Dessert Dish. 9¾″ long. A lovely, well-spaced design in underglaze blue, probably an exact copy of a Chinese original based on the lotus. The mark is imitation Chinese. *c.* 1760–65.

Plate 12. First Period Chestnut Basket, Cover and Stand. 10″ long. Twig handles of this kind are found upon many shapes and sizes of Worcester baskets, some with openwork trellis and others with solid sides, as are the flower-heads, in relief or merely painted forms. Painted in underglaze blue, and marked with open crescents. *c.* 1760–65.

Plate 13. First Period Tea-pot. 5½″ high. Here a Chinese style of decoration is reserved upon a powder-blue ground. That is, the white spaces were covered up while pigment in powdered form was blown upon the article, a Chinese process used for both blue-painted and polychrome wares, producing a granulated appearance. The piece bears two marks, the fretted square (or 'square mark') and the open crescent. *c.* 1760–65.

Plate 14. First Period Sweetmeat Stand. 5½″ high. Stands such as this, formed of scallop-shells upon bases made of small shells and seaweed, were made also at other factories, including Plymouth, Bow and Derby. While the underglaze blue flowers are of Meissen origin, the diapered borders are Chinese. *c.* 1760–65.

Plate 15. First Period Jug. 5¾" high. A graceful Worcester shape, featuring the 'mask lip' and with a serviceable loop handle and sensible foot-rim. The over-glaze black Hancock print, bearing the date 1757, represents Frederick the Great, and as usual it is accompanied by other prints of 'Fame' blowing two trumpets, and military trophies. In addition to the date, the print also carries the monogram RH (for Robert Hancock) and an anchor rebus for Richard Holdship (who left Worcester in 1764 to teach printing on porcelain at Derby) together with the word 'Worcester'.

Plate 17. First Period Sauceboat. 7½″ long. A model
of early origin, which was decorated in several ways,
in enamels, in underglaze blue or, as in this case, with
black overglaze prints, the leaves and flower sprays
enamelled. The prints are early examples of Hancock's
engraving. *c.* 1760.

Plate 16. First Period Chocolate Cup and Saucer.
This is a typical shape, the cup sometimes having
but one handle. The border is of hexagonal cell
diaper, and the floral subject is one of the commoner
Worcester printed designs, probably of Meissen deri-
vation. It is interesting to know that Chinese specimens are known upon which this kind of printed
design was laboriously copied in brushwork, a
reversal of the usual proceeding. Mark, a printed
letter R within a crescent. *c.* 1770.

Plate 18. First Period Vase and Cover. 13″ high. Here is Worcester overglaze black printing at its best, exquisitely detailed and sharp, and admirably fitted to the shape of the article. There are many versions of 'Panini Ruins', by which name these classical subjects are known. *c.* 1765.

Plate 19. First Period Round Dish. 10″ diam. An example of black printing to which a yellow ground colour, enamelling and gilding were added in the Giles London workshops. *c*. 1765.

Plate 20. First Period Jug. 9″ high. The characteristic mask-lipped, cabbage-leaf moulded jug, black-printed and enamelled over, with gilding. The print is after Francis Hayman's 'Mayday', and others not visible in the photograph are 'Rural Lovers' after Gainsborough and 'Milking Scene' after Luke Sullivan, all engraved by Hancock. *c*. 1765.

Plate 21. First Period Jug. 8″ high. The 'mandarin' style of pseudo-Chinese decoration, with panels or borders of diaper, and with a prominent black hair treatment, is very different from the style of decoration seen in Plates 23 and 24. It is effectively applied here to a cabbage-leaf jug. *c.* 1765.

Plate 22. First Period Tea Wares. The 'Queen Charlotte' or 'whorl' pattern is as a rule enamelled in red, blue and gold though variations are known which also feature sprays of green leaves and/or red berries. Late examples of Chinese porcelain are often found similarly decorated. Because the colours include underglaze blue we find that the pieces have square marks. *c.* 1765–70.

Plate 23. First Period Coffee-pot. 8¼" high. The 'feather pattern' moulding was an early one, over which the enamelling was applied regardless of the irregular surface. The subject, like that featured in Plate 24, is true Chinese. Notice the Worcester practice of painting tiny flower-sprays, birds, or insects in appropriate places. *c.* 1765.

Plate 24. First Period Leaf Dish. 8¼" long. Several forms of leaf-shaped dishes were made at Worcester, either in single or double, overlapping style, and decorated in every style according to period. This well-balanced, all-over pattern is usually called the 'Chinese Magician', and was probably a direct copy from a Chinese piece. Note the typical anglicization of the women and man. *c.* 1760–65.

Plate 25. First Period Tankard. 4⅝" high. The lovely bell shape is decorated with enamelled Japan style flowers upon a pale yellow ground, and the landscapes are in pink. Though the decoration is Chinese, the style is that of Meissen. *c.* 1765.

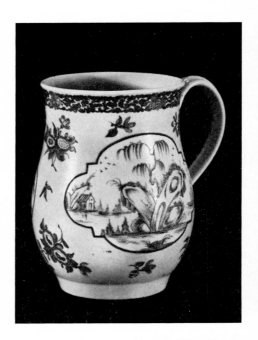

Plate 26. First Period Sauce Tureen. To be complete a tureen should have its cover, stand and ladle. This example is painted with the most splendid of all the Worcester 'Japan' patterns in underglaze blue, enamels and gold. In the 1769 Catalogue of the Worcester Works it is referred to as the 'Old Mosaick Japan' pattern. Marked with pseudo-Chinese symbols. *c.* 1770.

Plate 27. First Period Dish. 15½" long. The Worcester pierced edge, with applied flowers at the intersections, is here unusually enamelled in turquoise. The Kakiemon type flowers and prunus sprays alternate with panels of overglaze red (rouge de fer) patterned with gold, upon which are white chrysanthemum medallions. Similar patterns have underglaze blue panels instead of red ones. *c.* 1770.

Plate 28. First Period Tray. 6" diam. A plate form with typical twig handles, and applied flowers at the terminals. The colourful design is known as the 'Sir Joshua Reynolds' pattern, which is found with many different styles of border, and the bird rests upon a turquoise rock. It was taken from a Japanese rendering of a well-known Chinese design. *c.* 1770.

Plate 29. First Period Dessert Plate. 9″ diam. Such simple designs, brightly enamelled, are comparatively rare on our early porcelains, and in this case the reticent composition, enhancing yet not crowding the pure whiteness of the ware, is good enough to have been copied direct from the Oriental. *c.* 1765.

Plate 30. First Period Tea-bowl and Saucer. An example of the so-called 'Jesuit' style of decoration, pencilled in black enamel, not to be confused with black printing. The original 'Jesuit China' was decorated by a Chinese hand in the European style. *c.* 1760.

Plate 31. First Period Coffee-pot 9¾″ high. This pure Kakiemon decoration, perfectly spaced, is called the 'Partridge' or 'Quail' pattern, predominately red and gold in colour. The border is the most usual one to be found in conjunction with Kakiemon decoration. *c.* 1760–65.

Plate 32. First Period Dessert Basket. 11″ long. One of the several Worcester basket shapes, with the typical rope-twist handles, pierced sides, and applied flowers on the outside. The exotic birds reserved upon the scale-blue ground are in the style of the Sèvres painters Evans and Aloncle. Mark, a script W in underglaze blue. *c.* 1775.

Plate 33. First Period Round Dish.
10¼″ diam. An example of Giles
decoration, the birds painted with
a full, wet brush, and the fruits by
the 'sliced fruit painter'. *c.* 1770.

Plate 34. First Period Jug. 8¼″
high. A very lovely combination
of exotic birds and opaque apple-
green ground, thickly but carefully
applied, in order that the gilding
could almost touch it, but never be
applied over it. This was necessary
because for technical reasons the
gold would not 'take' on the green,
but had to be painted upon the
white-glazed surface *c.* 1775.

Plate 35. First Period Coffee-pot. 6″ high. A smaller type of Worcester coffee-pot, here with a yellow ground upon which is reserved a panel of naturalistic flowers painted in a very simple manner. A yellow ground colour was possibly used at Worcester in the early days, and it may vary in tone between lemon and sulphur. *c.* 1775.

Plate 36. First Period Basket. 7½″ long. A daring use of colour, the border being in turquoise, contrasting boldly with the enamels of the 'sliced fruit painter'. *c.* 1775.

Plate 37. First Period Vase and Cover. $11\frac{1}{2}''$ high. The hexagonal form was popular
during the First Period, more usually found decorated in underglaze blue than in
enamels. This outside decorated specimen features the beautiful but exceedingly rare
pink-scale ground which was derived from Meissen and introduced at Worcester as
early as 1761, after which date it was applied both inside the factory and, more often,
in outside studios. *c.* 1770

Plate 38. First Period Vase and Cover. 17½″ high. The graceful form of this piece is not obscured by the reticent decoration in 'dry blue' and gilding, in the Meissen style of naturalistic flower painting. The overglaze, bright blue enamel is always delicately and meticulously applied, as though with a single hair of the brush, and as a rule the flowers are botanically correct, though some are now no longer grown. This specimen is unmarked, but much 'dry blue' ware bears the Meissen crossed swords in underglaze blue. *c.* 1770–80.

Plate 39. First Period Salt Cellar. 2″ diam. Every collector would wish for nothing rarer than this specimen, which is in fact unique. It is clearly a silver shape, and the enamelled fruits are reserved upon a pea-green ground. *c.* 1770–75.

Plate 40. First Period Cake Plate. 7″ diam. A shape sometimes called a saucer dish, featuring a rich claret or ruby ground, and painting by the 'sliced fruit painter'. Notice the finely chased gilding which is a feature of claret ground pieces. The forerunners of the claret ground (which has often been faked, resulting in a muddy appearance very different from the purity of the authentic pigment) were the Meissen carmine pink, the Sèvres rose pompadour evolved in 1757, and the Chelsea claret first used in 1760. Many claret grounds were applied in the Giles workshops. *c.* 1770–75.

Plate 41. First Period Dessert Dish. 11½″ long. A very colourful dish from the 'Lord Henry Thynne' service, and a good example of the landscape painting which appeared during the last decade of the First Period. *c.* 1770–80.

Plate 42. First Period Dessert Dish. 11½″ long. Upon this piece the flowers are painted in the French style which replaced that of Meissen, between 1770 and 1780, and which in more formal manner is seen in the various 'hop-trellis' patterns. The festoons are typical, and the border is in 'French Green'. *c.* 1770–80.

Plate 43. First Period Jug. 10½″ high. Armorial porcelain of the First Period is comparatively rare, and this is a fine specimen, featuring beautifully drawn enamelled rustic scenes on either side, sprigs of Meissen flowers, and the colourful Arms of Brodribb with Berrowe in pretence. *c.* 1760–65.

Plate 44. First Period Vase and Cover. $11\frac{1}{2}$" high. There is a wide difference between the more sophisticated Chinoiserie of the 1770's and the simple 'Long Elizas' and mandarins of the early years. An example of the later work is here reserved upon a scale-blue ground. Square mark. *c.* 1770–75.

Plate 45. First Period Mug. 4⅝″ high. A pleasing, well-spaced example of Giles decoration in the Teniers style, with irregularly shaped, pink scale border. *c.* 1770.

Plate 46. First Period Vase. 10¾″ high. Upon the scale-blue of this rare specimen (the shape of which might suggest a later date) fine paintings of Cupids which are credited to John Donaldson are reserved. *c.* 1770.

Plate 47. First Period Tureen and Cover. 7½″ long. Partridge tureens of this kind, made in two sizes, were until 1949 thought to be Chelsea. They are found in white, with gilding, and in enamelled form, and though not exceedingly rare are nevertheless uncommon. A contemporary factory price card lists the enamelled version at 7 and 8 shillings. *c.* 1760–65.

Plate 48. First Period Vase. 10¾″ high. A graceful piece painted in underglaze mazarine blue, delicately gilded, with reserves containing animal subjects by O'Neale, entitled 'Leopards in an African Landscape' and 'Mars, Venus and Cupid'. The small oval panels contain bird paintings. Square mark. *c.* 1770.

Plate 49. First Period Tureen and Cover. 9½″ long. A well-moulded piece, with shell handles, decorated with animal subjects by Jefferyes Hamett O'Neale, whose name is spelt in different ways. O'Neale, known as the 'Fable Painter' because he chose Aesop's Fables as the source of much of his china-painting, probably worked for Giles, and he lived at Worcester between 1768 and 1770, perhaps working at the factory, though of this there is no proof. *c.* 1770.

Plate 50. Flights Plate. 9¾″ diam. From a splendid service made for the Duke of Clarence in 1792. The mercury gilding is of very fine quality, on a blue ground, and in the centre of each piece is a different painting by John Pennington of 'Hope on the Seashore'. Mark, FLIGHT in script, a crown above and an open crescent below, in underglaze blue. *c.* 1790.

Plate 51. Flights Card Tray. 9¾″ wide. Trays of this kind, sometimes called baskets, were made at Flights, Chamberlains and Graingers. The overlapping leaf border is gilded, and reserved on a pale green ground is a painting of a scene from 'Paul and Virginia', probably by Thomas Baxter. Inscribed on the base are the words 'The noise of the water frightened Virginia and she durst not wade through the stream'.

Printed mark of the Flight, Barr and Barr period. *c.* 1813–40.

Plate 52. First Period Group. 7″ high. The few figures made during the First Period are of such fine quality that one wonders why output was so restricted. Models known, in addition to this great rarity, are a Gardener and Companion, a pair of Turks, a Sportsman and Companion, and a 'La Nourrice'.

Plate 53. Flights Vase. 16¾″ high. The painting of splendid exotic birds continued into this later period, in this case with foliage and most elaborate mercury gilding. But for the mark, an open crescent and 'FLIGHT' in gold, one would be inclined to give a later date to this fine specimen. *c.* 1785.

Plate 54. Flights Vase. 9⅝" high. A perfect example of the best ornamental porcelain made at Flights, combining well-proportioned form, splendid mercury gilding, applied 'pearls' of white porcelain, and figure painting by Thomas Baxter. The painted scene is from 'King John' by Shakespeare, and on the base is the inscription, 'King John. Act IV Scene I. For heaven's sake, Hubert, let me not be bound.' Script mark, 'Flight Barr and Barr, Royal Porcelain Works, Worcester, London House, 1 Coventry Street.' *c.* 1813–40.

Plate 55. Flights Dessert Dish. 11" long. Shells or feathers appear on much Flights decorative ware, notably painted by Thomas Baxter. In this case, however, the shells are batt-printed in black. This process, which was capable of giving most delicate effects, was one in which the copper plate was oiled instead of inked, and the design transferred to the porcelain by means of a 'batt' or sheet of glue. The powdered colour was then sprinkled on. Impressed mark of the Barr, Flight and Barr period, 'B.F.B.' below a crown. *c.* 1807–13.

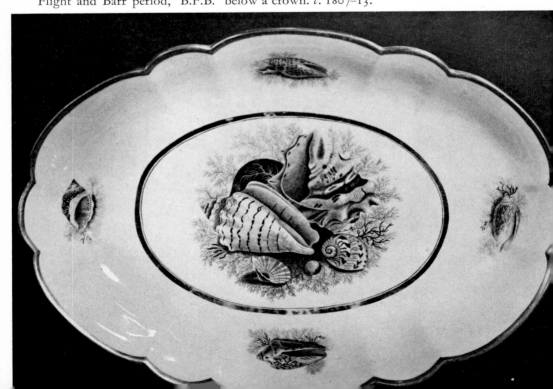

Plate 56. Chamberlains Vase and Cover. 10¾" high. The ground colour upon this handsome vase, made of the 'Regent' paste and restrained in its modelling, is salmon-pink, a favourite colour at the factory. Many later Worcester wares bear views of Worcester, but this one is interesting because it includes the Chamberlain Works. On the base the word 'Worcester' is inscribed, with the printed mark of the period. *c.* 1811–20.

Plate 57. Flights Vase and Cover. 9" high. Of comparable quality to the vase featured in Plate 54, and bearing the same mark, this specimen is painted with exotic birds by Davis reserved upon an underglaze mazarine blue ground. *c.* 1813–40.

Plate 58. Chamberlains Jug. $7\frac{1}{2}''$ high. The 'cabbage-leaf' mask-lip jug of early years was made throughout the Chamberlain period, and this specimen bears a view of Worcester Cathedral in sepia, painted by Humphrey Chamberlain. The flower-sprays are in gold. *c.* 1810–20.

Plate 59. Chamberlains Plate. $9\frac{5}{8}''$ diam. From a service made in 1816 for Prince Leopold of Belgium, bearing his Arms, and with a border of trophies, lions, eagles, palms and laurels reserved on a green ground. Printed mark.

Plate 60. Chamberlains Dish. 17″ long. From a service made for Princess Charlotte in 1816, finely painted with flowers and fruit, and with exotic birds by Davis, reserved on a pale blue ground. Printed mark of the period.

Plate 61. Chamberlains Armorial Poreclain. These pieces, from a breakfast service made for Lord Nelson in 1802, typify the most splendid armorial wares in which the factory specialized. Script mark, and pattern number 240.

Plate 62. Chamberlains Bowl. 4½″ high. Though lacking its cover, this well-modelled bowl is a suitable vehicle for Baxter's feather painting. The upper surface of the plinth is enamelled in pale blue. Script mark 'Chamberlain's Worcester'. *c.* 1810–20.

Plate 63. Chamberlains Cabinet Cup and Stand. Articles of this kind were not made for use but intended purely as cabinet pieces. They were accordingly most carefully decorated. The underglaze mazarine blue ground is patterned in gold vermiculated design and the painting, enclosed within raised and tooled gold scrollwork, is a view of Frogmore, according to the inscription on the base. Printed mark of the period. *c.* 1840–50.

Plate 64. Chamberlains Plate. 8½″ diam. The porcelain is here used purely as a canvas for fine specialized fruit painting by the versatile Thomas Baxter. Appropriately, the gilding is restrained. Printed mark. *c.* 1820.

Plate 65. Chamberlains Bowl and Cover. 9″ high. The well-modelled and gilded dolphins contrast effectively with the mazarine blue ground. The three oval reserves contain meticulously painted feathers by Baxter. Mark, 'Chamberlain's Worcester' in script. *c.* 1790–1800.

Plate 66. Chamberlains Pomade Pot and Cover. $4\frac{1}{8}''$ diam. The collector often sees such pots and lids in Pratt-ware, but a Worcester example is a rarity. On the cover is a coursing scene, and the various portions of the continuous landscape are named 'Going in and out Clever', 'Charging an Ox Fence', 'Swishing at a Rasper' and 'Going along a Slapping Pace'. 'Chamberlain' script mark. *c.* 1845.

Plate 67. Chamberlains Figure. 6″ high. Among the comparatively few figures made during the period was a set of five 'Tyrolean Singers', the brothers and sister Rainer, made in 1828. Mark, script 'Chamberlains Worcester'.

Plate 68. Graingers Figure Group. Though this interesting and finely modelled piece is unmarked, and would probably not be identified as Graingers porcelain on any evidence of style, its provenance is proved by its presence in one of the factory pattern books. It is in unglazed biscuit form, and may be dated *c.* 1850.

Plate 69. Chamberlains Card Tray. $13\frac{1}{2}''$ long. Whatever one's personal opinion of the border of applied shells, coral and seaweed, vividly enamelled, there can be no denying the technical perfection of this characteristic Chamberlain style of ornamentation. The view of the Houses of Parliament is extremely well painted, however unrelated to its frame. Printed mark for the period *c.* 1840–50.

Plate 70. Chamberlains Chalice. 8¾″ high. An early example of the perforated technique, in this case in a honeycomb form that was often used on still later Worcester wares, and perfected by George Owen in the 1890's. Mark, 'Chamberlain & Co., Worcester'. *c.* 1850.

Plate 71. Graingers Cabinet Cup and Saucer. A typical specimen of Graingers pierced work, enamelled, and richly gilt. *c.* 1860.

Plate 72. Graingers Vase. 9½″ high. Unmarked Graingers Worcester porcelain is often indistinguishable from that made in the two rival factories, and the likeness is very marked here. The panel of flowers upon a table, beautifully painted, is reserved upon a marbled green ground. Mark, 'Grainger Lee & Co. Worcester' in script. *c.* 1815.

Plate 73. Royal Porcelain Company Patera. $10\frac{1}{4}''$ diam. A lovely example of the 'Limoges Enamels' of Thomas Bott, in white upon a royal blue ground, done in 1867. Impressed mark of the Worcester Royal Porcelain Company.

Plate 74. Kerr and Binns Comport. $15''$ high. From the wonderful 'Shakespeare' or 'Dublin' service made for the Dublin Exhibition of 1853, and presented by a number of Irish noblemen to the Lord Lieutenant. The unglazed Parian figures were modelled by W. B. Kirk to represent Flute and Quince, characters in the 'Midsummer Night's Dream', and the two medallions of Tragedy and Comedy were painted by Thomas Bott. The fabulous creatures and cherubs heads of the dish are in white enamel upon a dotted gold ground.

Plate 75. Kerr and Binns Figure. 15″ high. A graceful specimen modelled in an ivory tinted paste, with delicate enamelling. It is named 'Venus rising from the Waves'. *c.* 1855–60.

Plate 76. Royal Porcelain Company Tray. 14½" diam. A brilliantly enamelled specimen, the brambles and oak-leaves in raised gold. The underside of the rim is bronze gilded. Date mark for 1881.

Plate 77. Kerr and Binns Dessert Plate. Made in Parian Ware, the embossed panels and border in ivory, blue and gold, and in the centre a print in black. K. and B. shield mark for the year 1858.

Plate 78. Royal Porcelain Company Dessert Plate. 9⅜″ diam. The same embossed shape, but pierced, was used in the Queen Victoria service. The birds, on a gold ground upon the rim within turquoise and gold scrolls, were probably painted by Hopewell. *c.* 1863.

Plate 79. Graingers Vase. 9¼″ high. The pilgrim flask shape was often used at Worcester during the latter half of the 19th century. On this piece the enamelled decoration is in Graeco-Italian style upon a matt cobalt blue ground. *c.* 1860–70.

Plate 80. Royal Porcelain Company Vase. 7⅜″ high. This horn-shaped specimen is known as the 'Rhyton Vase', and it is a perfect example of how effectively the glazed white Parian body combines with gilding. Date mark for 1878.

Plate 82. Royal Porcelain Company Shell Ornament. 15″ high. The perfected ivory paste was ideal to receive this kind of decoration, in this case in the Raphaelesque style. The modeller was J. Hadley, and the decoration was applied by Callowhill. *c.* 1870.

Plate 81. Royal Porcelain Company Group. 13″ high. In plain white form, whether biscuit or glazed, the beauty of a piece of porcelain depends solely upon good modelling. This group of 'Faust and Marguerite' was the work of W. B. Kirk. *c.* 1870.

Plate 83. Royal Porcelain Company Dessert Plate. 9¼″ diam. By this time, as the photographs clearly show, every porcelain shape was intended above all to act as a canvas for fine painting. The capable landscape and animal painting here was applied by R. Perling, and the pierced border is in gold and turquoise. Date mark for 1870.

Plate 84. Royal Porcelain Company Ewer. 11¾″ high. The gilded handle is in the form of an angel. The oval medallion, framed in gold 'beads', was painted by Josiah Rushton, and the tooled gilding applied by E. Bejot. The ewer form was very popular at Worcester at this time. Date mark for 1881.

Plate 85. Royal Porcelain Company Tea-pot. A duplicate of a part of the magnificent déjeuner service presented to the Countess of Dudley in 1865, magnificent although the porcelain is admittedly totally covered by decoration. The turquoise 'jewels' and 'pearls' by S. Ranford are upon a matt gold ground, and the classic head was painted by T. S. Callowhill. The date marks for 1876 and 1877 are upon the cover and body respectively.

Plate 86. Royal Porcelain Company Dessert Plate. 9¼″ diam. The decoration, by Luke Wells, was a revival of the Watteau style which was so often used upon much earlier English porcelains, though here the pierced rim and simple gilding are clearly indicative of the date of 1868 which is denoted by the mark.

Plate 87. Royal Porcelain Company Pair of Figures. 4″ high. In the Kate Greenaway style, well-modelled, though not in great detail. The girl on the left has a bronzed brown dress, and her companion has a pale yellow one. Date mark for 1885.

Plate 88. Royal Porcelain Company Candle Extinguishers. 3″ and 3 11/16″ high. Known as the 'Tichborne Candle Extinguishers', that on the right features Arthur Orton, a butcher, upon his block, who was the claimant, while the standing figure is Sir John Coleridge, counsel for the Trustees of the Tichbourne Estate. Coleridge may be fitted over Orton, thus extinguishing his claim.

Plate 89. Royal Porcelain Company Figure. 13″ high. The title of this model is 'The Health of the King', decorated in enamels with gilding upon a stained ivory ground. Date mark for 1898.

Plate 90. Royal Porcelain Company Vase and Cover. 23″ high. An extremely important example of the use of the ivory body with contrasting decoration in bronze and gold. Unmarked, but may be dated *c.* 1875–80.

Plate 91. Royal Porcelain Company Vase. 29½″ high. Though many have seen photographs of this piece or of its companion, few realize its importance, if only by reason of its considerable size. The two vases illustrate the art of the 16th century Italian potter. On the reverse side of this one is a representation of 'The Modeller', and the heads on the shoulders are of Maestro Georgio of Gubbio and Luca della Robbia of Florence. On the companion vase are modellings of 'The Painter' and 'The Furnace', with the heads of Michael Angelo and Raphael. The embossments are tinted and gilded, and the figures tinted in the well known Capo di Monti style. The artists responsible for the work were James Hadley and the Callowhill brothers. Date mark for 1878.

Plate 92. Royal Porcelain Company Candlestick. 8¾″ high. The Persian style in which this piece was modelled, by James Hadley, is somewhat too flamboyant for modern taste, though its technical excellence is obvious. The decoration in turquoise, black and blue was done by E. Bejot. Datemark for 1876.

Plate 93. Royal Porcelain Company Figure. 7⅝″ high. An interesting memento of the Boer War, entitle
'The Volunteer in Khaki', tinted in shades of brown with details in gold. Date mark for 1900.

Plate 94. Royal Porcelain Company Figures of Birds. These lovely life-like Bob White Quails were modelled by Dorothy Doughty and published in 1940 at a price of 275 dollars. They are part of a series of American birds, and the esteem in which they are held in the States is indicated by the fact that in 1967 a similar pair was sold for the sum of 37,000 dollars.

Plate 95. Royal Porcelain Company Vase and Cover. 13″ high. This is a remarkable example of the pierced or 'reticulated' work of George Owen, signed in the paste, and not to be confused with later work produced by semi-mechanical means. Date mark for 1916.

Plate 96. Hadleys Worcester Vase and Cover. 14″ high. This piece is typical of the wares produced at James Hadley's factory, which from 1896 until 1905 made its own characteristic porcelain, much of which bore coloured clay embellishments or mounts such as those to be seen in the photograph. In this instance they are coloured blue and buff. Monogram mark for the period 1900–02.

Plate 97. Royal Porcelain Company Equestrian Figure. 12″ high. This wonderful piece representing Her Majesty Queen Elizabeth II on the police horse Tommy was modelled by Doris Lindner on the occasion of Her Majesty's taking her first Trooping the Colour ceremony in 1947. One hundred were made, after which the moulds were broken, and it is intriguing to know that at Sotheby's, in February 1968, model number 92 was sold for £1,800.

Other books by the Author:

ENGLISH CERAMICS 1966

BRITISH POTTERY AND PORCELAIN 1962

COLLECTOR'S PROGRESS 1957

THE CHINA COLLECTOR'S GUIDE

THE DECORATION OF ENGLISH PORCELAIN 1954

ENGLISH BLUE AND WHITE PORCELAIN OF THE 18TH CENTURY 1947

Index

*(Numbers printed in **bold** face refer to plates)*

95